D1394252

Two Say Why

Two Say Why

Why I am Still a Christian

by

HANS URS VON BALTHASAR

and

Why I am Still in the Church

by

JOSEPH RATZINGER

Translated by
JOHN GRIFFITHS

Search Press
London

Franciscan Herald Press
Chicago

This translation first published in 1973 by
Search Press Limited, 85 Gloucester Road, London SW7 4SU

and

Franciscan Herald Press, 1434 West 51st Street, Chicago,
Illinois 60609

TWO SAY WHY: *Why I am Still a Christian*, by Hans Urs von
Balthasar, and *Why I am Still in the Church*, by Joseph Ratzinger,
translated from the German by John Griffiths (the original
appeared as Volume 57 of the *Münchener Akademie-Schriften* of the
Catholic Academy of Bavaria, published by Kösel-Verlag,
Munich). Library of Congress Catalog Card Number: 74–169057.
ISBN: 8199–0434–1 (USA). This translation Copyright © 1971 by
Franciscan Herald Press, 1434 West 51st Street, Chicago, Illinois
60609.

Nihil Obstat:
> Marion A. Habig O.F.M.
> *Censor Deputatus*

Imprimatur:
> Rt. Rev. Mgr. Francis W. Byrne
> *Vicar General, Archdiocese of Chicago*

September 22, 1971

Set in Intertype Baskerville,
printed in Great Britain by The Anchor Press Ltd,
and bound by Wm. Brendon & Son Ltd, both of Tiptree, Essex

ISBN 0 85532 289 6 (UK)

Contents

I

Why I Am Still a Christian

Hans Urs von Balthasar

1. Alpha

At one time the Church was more assured and convinced of its unique character and mission, and power to affect the world, than it has been ever since. Yet those were the very centuries when it was least concerned to examine its own nature and to define it theologically. Even Aquinas produced no special treatise on the Church, which was conceived as the ultimate form of all human society, ideally gathered together in the "kingdom" (more realistically, the Holy Roman Empire), and directed to the God from whom it derived. It was a "form" to be applied to the "matter" of humanity; the yeast whose savour was apparent only when mixed into "three bushels of meal" (though, of course, that was also the time when the Church's missionary activity was least evident).

With the dawn of the modern age, however, the secular sphere began increasingly to seek an independence which set it apart from the sacred. This process led eventually to the theory of "two social entities, each perfect in itself", one secular and the other spiritual, whose interests coincided only marginally. Of course this was also

the time when the Church could begin to see itself objectively – the spring-time of a largely institutional
ecclesiology. This seems at first to have been as inevitable as the liberation of the secular sciences from their
sacral strait-jacket. Yet in recalling today the disciples'
original mission to all nations, the function of the Christian community as leaven, and the former ideal of a
secular-cum-spiritual "Christendom", the second Vatican
Council has again acknowledged that the "Church" (as
"form") essentially transcends the world (as "matter").
It has thrown the doors wide open yet reminded Christians of their basic apostolic duty.

It seems somewhat romantic – this dream of refur-
bishing the medieval ideal in a wholly different situation :
a desacralized world suspicious of and fundamentally an-
tagonistic to a fossilized, self-enclosed Church; even
more so when the attempt is to be made by a constantly
dwindling band of Christians on behalf of a self-suffi-
cient world perfecting itself under its own steam. Yet
the first disciples had to contend with a pagan world-
civilization and the political and military security of an
immense area. No less utopian a dream, in fact. But in
little more than two hundred years that immensity had
been Christianized.

Admittedly, in those years an invincible, intensive force
was at work : one utterly convinced of its uniqueness and
ability to win through. But what conviction has Vatican
II shown in sending its renewed Christians out into the
world? Do they trust in the formative power of the pri-

mitive Church? Doesn't this power have to be still greater
and yet emerge as an even more concentrated force from
a single emission point, precisely because the world on
which it is to be focussed is more complex, pluralistic
and self-contradictory than any ancient civilization could
ever have been?

In fact, Christian missionaries are asked to do something almost superhuman: they are required to change
from a static and self-enclosed to a dynamic and apostolic
Church which has both the power of unity (without
which it could have no unifying effect) and the ability to
expand into the diversity of this world (without which it
could not hope to penetrate the world as it is).

This is a programme for supermen: one that seems
in every way beyond the scope of mere human beings,
especially when we remember that the power of unity,
from which everything is to flow, is the power of the
crucified and powerless man who renounced the means
of power of this world, whereas the world possesses an
ever-growing arsenal of powerful aids to conquer human
problems and unify the world.

Perhaps I should use the word "saints" instead of
"supermen", while attributing to them certain new
human dimensions: of being both in the power of the
source of all things and wholly at the utmost point of
its outpouring; of being wholly with the crucified Lord
and wholly with the human creatures whose need and
God-forsakenness Jesus shared to the point of identification. Of course they wouldn't have to be in two places

at once; if they kept the right tension between the two locations, they would be in only one place. Then they would be doing exactly what a Christian life and mission demand, and consequently would not need constantly to worry how it ought really to be done, and whether men were in fact capable of such a task anyway.

This is important. Just as Christian faith in what God did for the world through Jesus can never be fully explained in rational terms (if it were possible to do so, I would have understood this or that act of God, and then it would no longer be an act of God for us), so the Christian existence that is lived by virtue of that faith can never locate itself definitively in relation to that faith. It aspires to be an expression of that faith and therefore contained in and formed by it. It does not have to trouble itself with the insoluble problem of exactly what my relationship as a failure and sinner is to the Lord whom I proclaim and somehow represent : with the problem of exactly what distance and closeness mean in this relationship. It doesn't have to worry about an even more difficult problem referred to by Paul : What is my relation to the Christ-event?

Do I stand *before* the cross (which I always have to aim for first of all), or *in* the cross and death itself, or *after* the cross in the resurrection (which first makes possible my taking part in the Christ-event)? Which Lord do I approach in the eucharist? The eternal Lord who will never die again? Or the one who suffers his agony until the world's end, and whose death I show forth in every celebration of the eucharist? Or do these two modes of existence merge indistinguishably, for the Lamb is upon God's throne, simultaneously living and "as though slain from the beginning of the world"?

The mystery of Christian existence derives its strength from faith in the mystery of Christ; therefore it is impenetrable, and no Christian who has any real claim to be one will try to elucidate it. His existence is marked out by two fixed points : that is from which he lives, and that towards which he lives. The first is God in Christ; the second is his fellow man. He himself can be a Christian only by existing as the movement between those essential points : a transition by the Holy Spirit.

Everything depends on correct discernment of the alpha point, which holds the concentrated unifying force that must spread out into the pluralism of the world. The alpha certainly does not consist of me and of my actions. My behaviour can only bear witness to what preceded my self and has now confronted and affected me. I shall be concerned with this alpha alone in the following pages – with its properties and the evidence it offers of its originality. The justification for my remaining a Christian depends on the cogency of this evidence.

The point towards which we look is the grain of mustard seed in the parable. It is smaller, more insignificant and poorer than all the other seeds. It is merely "sown upon the ground", never displayed as a cultivated growth but apparent only in the process of dying (decay) and resurrection as ear and fruit. No contemplative "aesthet-

ics" can penetrate this "drama" of the mustard seed;
the most fundamental thing we can see is always what
happens (apparently of itself) between God and the
world. But the primary subject of this happening "of
itself" is always God. Whatever happens is what *he* does
and suffers : in the man Jesus Christ, and through him
for and in all men.

All subsequent problems have always to be related to
this foregoing dramatic point, however important they
may be as direct consequences of the principle. The question is not, therefore, one concerning the relation of
the Christian alpha to others that have arisen in the course
of world history and also claim to be the starting-point.
Nor is it why I belong to any one Christian denomination
rather than another. Nor the question of the prerequis-
ites that are demanded of the Church and of the world
before the mustard seed bears fruit.

Such questions would raise the problems of adaptation,
aggiornamento, hermeneutics, demythologization, and
commitment to modern society. But however much such
problems fire us, they take second place to the one before
us now. The first question is not *How can I appear as a
credible Christian today?* but *Why am I still a Christian?*

This is where it is really important to keep the questions in proper order. The post-conciliar confusion has
come about largely because the Council thought that the
main questions the trinitarian and christological dogmas,
and the dependent ecclesiology) could be taken as a
basis without more ado, and that they could start straight

into the pastoral problems arising from that basis. Perhaps this kind of procedure is permissible in a number of secular areas. It is inappropriate in Christianity, where the river can never be divided from its source.

No beta can be explained other than in terms of its alpha. The alpha always presupposes everything else, yet we can never take it for granted as a premiss just to be left behind us, like that. If we take it for granted, then – like the builders of the tower of Babel – our discourse is confusion and we cannot even say what everyone knows. The common task, begun in dialogue, is left incomplete; and each man goes his own way.

2. The Challenge

The essence of Christianity may be summed up by using one of the later "I am" pronouncements (which Jesus probably never spoke himself); they are verbal expressions of the challenge that Jesus lived in his actual existence : "I am the way...".

Buddha and Mahomet might well have asserted that they were the way to the truth, which they had learned through a special revelation and were now able to point out to others. But "I am the truth" is a very different kind of assertion. In fact, it doesn't matter which concept of truth is in question : the Old Testament Semitic notion or the Greek one. What is intended is much more than some truth that happens to rank above all others in the universe; and more than the sum of all the true propositions that can be asserted about everything we find in the universe.

What is intended is something embracing all philosophic truths and which alone endows such truths with the property of truthfulness. Because the speaker says "I", his assertion of all-embracing truth is no reference to a mere rational truth. By his assertion he has already transcended any possible antithesis between factual truth and truth founded on reason. He transcends the very transcension of his assertion if he then says: "I am the life".

He is speaking here of life pure and simple, not of the life principle invested and restructured in individual living beings, but of the inexhaustible divine source that transcends that principle: what is often, in the same context, described as "light"; the light of life which, for Plato and for Fichte in his later period, lies above the area of being and truth; the goal that offers fulfilment beyond all striving; the happiness that delights beyond all true knowing.

The "I" that says, in this instance, "I am", is elevated, as that light and goal, above every human I–thou relationship, not as if it were a mere "mediation" of human freedoms and dialogues, but so as to make possible and open up the ways between two as *the* way of both, and the truths between them as *the* truth of both.

There is an immense provocation here which is unique in world history and seems almost absurd, coming as it does from a single individual, and therefore a minute fragment of the universe with all its multitudinous ways and truths – and from an individual, too, who the very night before he died claimed the power of eternal life.

If we allow the speaker to take the responsibility for what he claims, and do not put it down to the enthusiasm of the author of the fourth gospel; if we see his assertion as the sum total of a wholly demanding life that had persisted in refusing confinement within a fixed framework and saw itself as continuous with the great things God did in Israel, and as consummating, not contradicting, those acts, then it is obvious that no human wisdom (which always tries to understand the things of this world in terms of an all-comprehensive framework) could endure this kind of provocation – or has been able to stand it since its first enunciation.

The Greek mind found it ridiculous that one of the products of all-pervasive *physis* should equate itself with the generative matrix. Jewish thought found it even more incredible that a created man should predicate of himself the attributes proper to the creator of the world and the covenant-Lord of Israel. It is still nonsense (but now to a modern evolutionary universal philosophy of any persuasion) to assert that one wave in the river that has flowed for millions of years and will continue to flow unthinkingly for yet more millions once the wave is no more, can be identified with the river; nonsense, too, to assert (especially when mankind is entering upon an age of maturity and of future self-determination) that this wave has already comprehended all that future, and enclosed within itself the fulness of time and of the end of time.

On attempting to estimate the degree of provocation in such fantastic claims, we see clearly that any school of religious or philosophic thought must be deeply shocked by and surprised at another statement in the same context : "They hated me without cause."

3. Relative Singularities

Any philosophy that tries to see reality as a whole will tend to refuse any identification of a part with the whole. Yet it might admit so presumptuous a claim to some extent in trying to show that significant aspects of reality as a whole may (for the first time perhaps) become concentrated in the contingent part (which, as such, is open to inspection by the rational mind). The historical event may be a significant concentration of the whole.

It is not difficult to affirm the temporal contingency of the Jesus-event. Modern scholarship is uncovering more and more evidence of ways of thought and events of that time. The results of this research are increasingly accepted and put forward as a matter of course.

The *aggiornamento* programme, in all the difficulties experienced in trying to put it into practice, shows very clearly how firmly the gospel truths are attached to that point in time, and how hard it is for us to translate the Gospel into more accessible images and categories, even though we realize how the expressions are conditioned by their own age and perhaps sense their supra-temporal meaning.

On the other hand, the universal significance of the Jesus-event, beginning with the moment at which he entered history, can be described all the more reliably because Jesus himself spoke to posterity, promised his own divine Spirit to his faithful disciples, and (according to Luke) fulfilled this promise on the day of Pentecost.

Since then, the Church, as the community of men reconciled with God in the Holy Spirit and given God's life and light, has mediated to the world something that in Jesus is at first alien and unique, in such a way that this unique something seems analogous to other relatively singular things that have emerged in history. Let us look for a moment at three forms of singularity.

1. Great works of art appear like inexplicable miracles and spontaneous eruptions on the stage of history. Sociologists are as unable to calculate the precise day of their origin as they are to explain in retrospect why they appeared when they did. Of course works of art are subject to certain preconditions without which they cannot come into being: such conditions may be effective stimuli but do not provide a full explanation of the work itself.

Shakespeare had his predecessors, contemporaries and models; he was surrounded by the atmosphere of the theatre of his time. He could only have emerged within that context; yet who would dare offer to prove that his emergence was inevitable? Mozart's *Magic Flute* was preceded by a number of Viennese and Italian suggestions and models; there was a considerable amount of material available, but no one can explain the unique form that became manifest in this material.

At most, we can point to or guess at the propitious moment – the *kairos* – but never whatever it is that flows in it and gives it that lasting form which, as soon as it emerges, takes control. *It speaks the word*. Its unique utterance becomes a universal language.

A great work of art is never obvious and immediately intelligible in the language that lies ready to hand, for the new, unique language that comes into existence with it is its interpreter. It is "self-explanatory". For a moment the contemporary world is taken aback, then they understand, and begin to speak in the newly minted language (e.g. "the age of Shakespeare") as though they had invented it themselves. The unique word makes itself comprehensible through its own self. The greater a work of art, the more extensive at least the cultural sphere it dominates will be.

The Magic Flute is known to every child who hums the Papageno arias, but even a really fastidious ear never tires of hearing it : the Pamino recitative, the Tamina aria, the farewell trio all represent inexhaustible mystery.

A great work of art has a certain universal comprehensibility but discloses itself more profoundly and more truly to an individual the more attuned and practised his powers of perception are. Not everyone picks up the unique inflection of the Greek in a chorus of Sophocles, or of the German of *Faust*, Part II, or of the French of a poem by Valéry. Subjective adaptation can add something of its own, but that objective adequacy which is able to distinguish the noble from the commonplace is more important.

Philosophies of art – Schelling's and Hegel's, for example – try to project the great, irrationally and arbitrarily erupting works of art and the picture of the world they adduce against a horizon of universal understanding. And is there any reason why they should not partially succeed? Yet the "miracle" that is a great work of art remains inexplicable.

2. *Genuine love between persons* is probably less common than one thinks – although most men believe that they have some share in it, and that they really possess it for brief moments. It may well be as rare as great works of art, which tower here and there above the mass of what masquerades as art.

I am not thinking about the mischance of passion which, as in the *Tristan and Isolde* of Gottfried and of Wagner, relates the whole world to this one absolutely fixed point, and with it gives itself up to disaster, but about something that is much simpler and that to succeed requires a Christian predisposition : a dedication of one's whole life to a "thou" in whom the lover sees illumined the quality of the absolute, which involves the whole world.

Such dedication is a wager that makes sense in the end only if related to an absolute venture : the apparently arbitrary choice by God of Israel from among all other nations (Deut. 7, 7) and the consequence – the call of Jesus and no other.

The glory of loving choice by God raises the individual, lost in the anonymity of the species, to the uniqueness of a person. In this ultimate mutual awareness between two lovers, Eros can not merely offer the intial impulse, but continue the whole way, if only it allows itself to be purified into transfigurations beyond itself : Dante and Beatrice, Hölderlin and Diotima, Claudel's *Silver Slipper*, Teilhard's *Hymn to Beatrice*.

There is a pure foretaste in the *Alcestis* of Euripides. Line 242 and the following tell of the vicarious death of the wife for her husband who, at the moment of farewell, knows that he will live on, lonely upon the earth : "If you die, I live no longer : you are my life and my death, for your love is holy to me" (lines 277–9).

In *The Meaning of Sexual Love* (1892–1894) Soloviev praised so sublime love that even subtle reason cannot explain it. In the eyes of the world it always looks like folly, for the stream of life flows on (Hofmannsthal has described the immanent "wisdom" of this "unfaithfulness" in many ways); it sets itself deliberately and stubbornly against the current laws of life; and somehow it interprets itself eschatologically : in the midst of time this love discovers not only a "moment" of eternity, but a lasting experience of faithfulness that rises forever above all immanence.

3. That which is seldom achieved by love is offered as a possibility to every man in the moment of his death,

when he comes to understand himself not merely as a transitory individual in the ever-flowing stream of life – "to yield oneself up to which is delight" – but as a unique person who has to carry out his own unique commission against a finite, and not merely limited, horizon, and who in the end cannot do so.

It is this extreme loneliness of dying that makes the individual who, unlike the animals, sees what is ahead, conscious of his own personal uniqueness. On this point Scheler (*Death and Afterlife*, 1911–1912) and Heidegger are correct. Although the biblical revelation stresses more the spiritual solidarity of all men, thus introducing something like a corporate human history that is supra-individual (though not cosmic and cyclical in style), nonetheless it makes is thoroughly aware, under both the old and the new covenants, in contrast to the idea of solidarity, of the finitude of personal life in face of the loneliness of personal death.

When one leaves the society of men and walks towards the judgment of the God who predestines; when one enters that refining fire, through which the individual must pass, and in which the worth of his deeds upon earth will be revealed – empty straw or solid metal (I Cor. 3, 12 ff) – one walks completely alone.

Here, in earnest, it is *"monos pro monon"*; there can be no quick reference to the merits of others. Here no one can take my place: "Each will be rewarded according to his deeds" (Ps. 62, 13; Prv. 24, 12; Sir. 35, 24; Mt. 16, 27; Rom. 2, 6; I Cor. 4, 5; II Cor. 5, 10).

At the judgment the communion of saints can be understood only dialectically, in conjunction with this appointed loneliness. Death and judgment are primarily an interruption of every horizontal, dialogic situation; all such situations derive their meaning only from a non-dialogic situation, from one that answers to God alone.

From this we must conclude logically that true time is primarily the one each individual counts from his death and judgment, whereas common "world-historical" time, made into a chronological continuum by bracketing-off personal deaths, is a secondary phenomenon, because in it the whole motive that constitutes the seriousness of temporality is suspended.

A philosophy of the future, which takes account of the whole ethos of man in the time to come when he himself will have gone, can address man only as a member of a species and not as a person. The problem of how the individual person can incorporate into his finite time any notion of mankind's future ultimately demands a christological answer.

I have picked out three points at which at least a relative singularity stands out from environing human reason. These points have not been systematically arranged, but merely displayed as symptoms. They do, however, have something in common. Man is always confronted by a sheer datum, acceptance of which determines his rational attitude towards it.

In order objectively to perceive and then judge the

unique work of art, he has to create for himself the appropriate mode of receptivity.

In order to love, he has to discover in the beloved a value presented to him, which may perhaps be for him alone to see and to come forward and receive.

In order to approach his death responsibly, he has to accept this frontier and adapt his actions to conform to it.

At these three points we find a provocation offered by the several types of uniqueness, in that each eludes the law of generality.

As Paul says: "Not that it makes the slightest difference to me whether you, or indeed any human tribunal, find me worthy or not . . . the Lord alone is my judge" (I Cor. 4, 3 f). Yet all three situations are phenomena belonging to the general, human, mundane sphere.

They bear a dialectical relationship to the universal that finds expression in a certain secrecy, defencelessness, and often shyness. The true artist, aware of his own worth, doesn't boast about his work, but leaves it to its fate. It may be carried on high in triumph, or it may remain in the shadows (Schubert) only to be exhumed later, as if by chance. Great personal love can remain esoteric; and the responsibility that comes from facing death is always silent. Whatever is aware of its own uniqueness surrenders itself unhesitatingly to relativity.

4. Absolute Singularity

This modest action of the sublime would seem to be eclipsed at the point where a man, Jesus of Nazareth, claimed that he was the way, the truth, and the life. The fact that the claim was made with modesty, or rather with humility – "I am meek and lowly of heart" – in no way weakens it, but makes it seem all the more unusual.

He is represented as the one who is absolutely singular or unique: "No one has gone up to Heaven except the one who came down from Heaven, the Son of Man who is in Heaven" (Jn. 3, 13). And the thought is echoed by his disciple: "A spiritual man, on the other hand, is able to judge the value of everything, and his own value is not to be judged by other men" (I Cor. 2, 15).

This is said loudly and clearly. Would a wise man raise his voice in this way? Do the wise not speak more softly? And what of the constant stress on his own boldly pronounced "I"? "It was said of old to your fathers, but *I* say to you." The whole Gospel is full of this resounding *I*. We cannot shut our ears to it.

People would like to turn Jesus into an apostle of love

of one's neighbour standing up for the poor and the oppressed, and declaring his solidarity with sinners. But then they would have to take away all his provocative references to his own person, and all his measuring of others by their relationship to him: 'If anyone . . . is ashamed of me and of my words, the Son of Man will also be ashamed of him when he comes in the glory of his Father . . ." (Mk. 8, 38).

It is immaterial whether they distinguish the "I" from the Son of Man. They would have to excise the provocation in the question: "Who do people say I am . . . who do you say I am?" (Mk. 8, 27 ff), and the command to leave all "for my sake" (Mk. 9, 29) immediately and without first fulfilling the basic duties of piety (Mk. 8, 21 f). All these words and actions are characterized by a severity comparable in love and behaviour with nothing else that can lay claim to greatness in the history of man.

A man who presents himself in this way, must realize the extent of the demands he is making. The disputes with the Jews, reported by John, are one long relenting provocation. A man who uses such peremptory tones must be resigned to and prepared for anything. He must have some weapon that gives him the confidence to challenge the whole world. He must be conscious that he is able to step forward with complete authority.

At the centre of history, he knows himself to be the one who includes all things from beginning to end: "Before Abraham was, I am." "You will see the Son of Man coming." "I am the alpha and the omega." He must see clearly that in him the End, the *eschaton*, is in sight.

But how can he be the End if he stands, a mortal man, within the stream of history, which will flow on after his death? He will have to make the apparently mad claim that the outrunning of his own death embraces the outrunning of all history to its very end; that he possesses finite time in such a powerful and primary sense that it holds within itself all past aeons of time – emptied of death.

If he is correct, something equally crazy has to happen: all that he is, his life and death taken together, manifests itself as the absolute. Death is essentially part of this manifestation, for speaking and acting and even suffering do not reveal the whole truth about his being. But if the claim stands, the whole truth must also possess an *absolute weight* that can be counterbalanced by nothing, and – because it is a question of truth – be able to show that this is so.

The stone in one pan of the scales must be so heavy that one can place in the other all the truth there is in the world, all religion, all philosophy, every complaint against God, without counterbalancing it. Only if that is true is it worthwhile remaining a Christian today.

If there were any weight capable, ever so slightly, of raising up the Christian side of the scales, and moving it into the sphere of relativity, then being a Christian would become a matter of preference, and one would have to reject it unconditionally. Somehow or other it would be outflanked. To think of it as of more than historic interest would be a waste of time.

The Gospels are full of disturbing miracle stories. A man does not prove his authenticity by working miracles. Truth must be its own proof. But how could Jesus' claim prove itself if his life has still not reached the end of the world and of time, if the proof will be conclusive only when all life and death has run its course?

Miracles are in themselves no proof of what really matters; but they can be signs in a twofold sense : signs that what was intended from the beginning – the eschatological "miracle" of God which breaks the very bounds of human reason – has come to be in Jesus Christ, has started to happen; and second, that in its consummation the event, if it occurs, must be so conclusive in the one really needful thing, that all mundane understanding is put right out of joint and appears to that understanding as "miracle".

5. The Eschatological Moment: Its Form

We could try to use the Christ-event to plumb all reality to the utmost limits of thought. All, God and the world, would be bound to converge on this centre. The world would find its ultimate essence in its self-transcendence through the Son of God, and God would manifest himself as all in all, by presenting himself above the Son of God, who is the head of the "body of the Church" and ultimately of the whole world, as the meaning of all becoming, and as the one who realizes all his creative potential.

Nothing could be left out of this all-embracing principle; one would in the end define absolute truth as the identity of identity (God) and of non-identity (the world distinct from God); and would be aware that from this formula only non-being – i.e. nothing – could apparently be excluded.

In terms of the Christ-event, no matter how "free" God's self-revelation in Christ may seem to be, God remains the absolute reality, but now has become visible, knowable and accessible to thought. Whoever has grasped the absolute with his mind has – essentially – grasped everything.

Remember those two post-Hegelians: Kierke-gaard who (in Protestant style) in his "absolute paradox" summed up the patristic axiom, *"si compre-hendis, non est Deus"*; and Marx who, from an alleged intellectual grasp of God, drew the correct conclusion that it is sheer and self-destructive speculation to say that the mind of the thinker has explored everything, because truth lies not in thinking but in the world-changing action that man retrieves from the estrangement of his thoughts. Both are right: absolute philosophy is not the last word, for it has grasped God but not changed the world.

If Christianity is to possess eschatological momentum, is to have the last word, it must prove its claim in a special way, so that at no point does it "explain" the mystery that is God – even though God reveals himself therein – but at the decisive point actively changes the world.

First: the provocation contained in the assertion "I am the way, the truth, and the life" cannot be watered down by compromise. There is nothing quite like this statement; it is unique at the centre of history. Every-thing is founded upon this utterly simple point. It does not come from a combination or synthesis of Jewish and Hellenistic expectations. It is completely unexpected and incapable of being expected; and where it suddenly appears, without allowing a moment's pause for reflec-tion, it immediately demands belief: "I am the resur-rection and the life. Do you believe this?" (Jn. 11, 25 f). The answer is "Yes"; and faith has to recognize the validity of the claim sufficiently in the claim itself to allow of assent.

But it would not be faith if it were able to work out this validity in a rational system and expound it exhaustively. There must always be something which eludes or obstructs faith when it thinks that it is about to understand the conditions for the possibility of the reality that stands before it. When Jesus says: "I am the truth", "I am the resurrection", he is saying that God is present in him. But: *"Si comprehendis, non est Deus"* – if you understand it, it is not God. If God shows himself in Jesus Christ, then Anselm's formula for God applies to this manifestation too: *"id quo majus cogitari non potest"* – that than which a greater cannot be conceived.

The context makes it clear that this means neither exhaustive knowledge – as though we could conceive the *maximum*, the all-embracing system of truth – nor a dynamic-comparative knowledge – as though the objective, utter "greaterness" of God corresponded to a subjective, ever-expanding thought in man. It is rather that the *"majus"* – greater – of the one who manifests himself takes possession of the *"cogitatio"* – thinking – in such a way that the latter, by acknowledging its being over-mastered, praises the perfect victory of the inscrutable truth of God.

Other formulas of Anselm confirm this interpretation: *"videt se non plus posse videre"* – it sees that it cannot see more: the little eye can encompass only so much, although the object seen extends farther than its power of vision; and the eye (in being overmastered) terms this farther field of vision *"quiddam majus quam cogitari possit"* – something greater than could be thought. And so we come to the ultimate formulations which open up vision into a higher sphere, without allowing what is seen there to be dragged down into the realm of sight: *"evidentissime comprehendi potest, ab humana scientia comprehendi non posse"* – it can most clearly be comprehended that it cannot be comprehended by human knowledge. Or yet again in other words: *"rationabiliter comprehendit incomprehensibile esse"* – he reasonably comprehends that it is incomprehensible.

In order to express these formulas in a practical manner, we may again ask: Can anyone, with eye or ear completely exhaust a great work of art? It offers itself totally for us to take, and yet in so doing eludes total understanding. This is even more true of the beloved who yields himself up freely and yet always stays out of final reach. And who has fathomed death, which intensifies the light of finality that shines upon each day of our lives, and gives them definition?

These three spheres, in their several ways, show what can be meant by "grace". That there is a thing so magnificent as a work of art, which offers itself ungrudgingly to me, can make itself intelligible to me by some intrinsic power of communication, while remaining in a sphere penetrated by my conceptual categories; that there is something so improbable as a "thou", which, for no comprehensible reason, has chosen me from among all beings as the object of his love and devotion; that there is an inescapable end of life, which out of an incomprehensible mercy grants me the privilege of yet another today among the living : this is grace.

At every point the essential thing is that that which is conferred by grace can be comprehended as such, but can never be logically reconstructed in retrospect. I cannot say : that is what I have always "really" expected, or what my mind and heart have always been oriented towards, so that only the slightest impulse from outside was required to allow my pre-understanding to crystallize into perfect insight.

That which offers itself with the basic character of grace can never be grasped rationally without losing that distinctive quality. And in so far as it can never be captured it constitutes a continuous source of bliss for the recipient.

Nor is that which grace gives ever in the last analysis something *given* : it remains within the originating act of that which gives itself. It keeps on producing meaning out of itself, and this prevents understanding from closing in upon the meaning already revealed. On the contrary, the more meaning that is revealed, the more *faith* the recipient is able to put in that which gives itself.

These affirmations lead us back from the approximations to our main object. This embraces certain aspects of our three analogies, but is much more than a clever combination of them. It is the "glory" which was quite unimaginable and which graciously invites us to share in itself. It is the gift that is quite undeserved, the gift of absolute love that turns towards me. And from the angle of judgment upon my life, it is the grace of patience and clemency. All of these, however, are only formal statements that must now be tested and filled with content.

6. The Eschatological Moment: Its Content

Everything is founded upon the claim that Jesus made. This claim is the stone that is thrown into the pool, sending out concentric circles of waves. The last circle, always clearly linked to the generating centre, spreads out to embrace the most distant shore.

It is enough to consider three circles in succession : the Jesus-event itself; Biblical revelation as a whole; the overflowing of this revelation into the whole history of mankind : "You will be my witnesses not only in Jerusalem but throughout Judaea and Samaria, and indeed to the ends of the earth" (Acts 1, 8). Are we to say that we, who live in the ambit of the third circle, can see the origin only through a multiplicity of estranging media, so that we are obliged to undertake a long series of hermeneutic manipulations in order to arrive after several transpositions and by way of conjecture at the original meaning of the first circle?

If that were so, the claim to be the eschatological moment – for all times and places – would already have been thoroughly refuted. The claim, along with the whole scandal it contains, must be powerful enough (and this power is the Holy Spirit) to make itself intelligible "always, until the end of the world" and "to all nations". This is not to deny the part played by hermeneutics ("you will be my witnesses" and "teach them to observe all things", which includes, presumably, teaching them to understand). But the claim, if justifiably upheld, is not dependent on hermeneutical acuity.

a. *The first circle: the Christ-event.* Everything depends on the claim made by Christ. This claim cannot be interpreted out of existence. Humility serves only to underline its strangeness. It can only present a challenge; and this is precisely what it did the moment it was made.

In the third chapter of Mark's Gospel we find Jesus regarded by his disciples as mad, by the scribes as possessed of a devil (vv. 21–2); and the scribes have already made up their minds that this intolerable person must die (3, 6). In the eyes of the *cognoscenti* the claim could only appear as *hubris,* no matter how much the crowd was impressed by Jesus' eloquence and miracles, and although Jesus counted himself one of the line of prophets that ended in John the Baptist (Mt. 5, 12, etc.).

But the scandal of his "I" sayings is of quite a different kind from that of the prophets. The cross is the compensating justification for arrogance, and the fact that the one convicted felt, as his cry of abandonment shows, that God, too, was judging him, corroborates the justice of the verdict. (The presumption of the closeness of his "I" to the "I" of Yahweh is compensated by apparent remoteness.)

The fate of the Galilean seems to hang in the balance between these two moments. And then, on the third day after his burial, the dead man meets his disciples as one alive. No one could have expected this, not even in an age used to the notion of the resurrection of the dead on the last day – a day that was not far off.

The resurrection of one man, who thereby had arrived at the end of the world, in contrast to all the others who would go on living in time, threw every concept of time – even the apocalyptic notion – into confusion. They just could not believe it : they must have seen a spirit.

It was possible that Jesus' precise announcements concerning his coming resurrection were retrospective interpolations – that remained to be seen. The event certainly could not have been expected, for, as things were, there was no concept available with which to frame the thought. This is obvious from the way in which the attempt is made immediately to adapt it to current ideas : if one man has arrived at the end of the world, that means that the end of time really has dawned, and the resurrection of the rest – or, what is the same thing, the return of the risen Lord – is at hand. This interpretation proved to be a delusion.

The time-horizon of Jesus of Nazareth was obviously not that of the rest of mankind. It was part of his commission, and hence of his claim, completely to encompass the history of this world within the scope of his mortal life. His finite span of life hid within itself the life-span of all who had died in the past and of all who would die in the future: here, in one single instance, primary, personal time has become identified with all the time that has run in the course of history. But who at that time could understand this? Luke sets a limit to every attempt: "It is not for you to know times or dates that the Father has decided by his own authority" (Acts 1, 7).

The extension of chronological time removes the Easter-event more and more from the sphere of time-conditioned apocalypticism. But from the very start – as John frequently confirms (16, 8) – it was understood that, with the resurrection of the condemned man, God in his righteousness had taken a stand at his side (Acts 2, 36). The monstrous claim has been justified and corroborated. And if the claim made by Jesus could be made only in the consciousness that it would be repaid with total rejection by, and excommunication from, Israel (that is, with complete disaster), the cross, too, was justified.

The whole man Jesus (and a man consists of all that he attempts in life and his destruction in death) became hidden within the eternal life of God. In other words: not merely what a man does, but also what he suffers, is of value in the sight of God. A man does not have first to be purified from his shame and helplessness and frailty before he can move out into the absolute. Just as he is – a failure, and abandoned by God – so is he received. His scars are accepted not only as authentication, but as enablement.

The Gospels are written from the viewpoint of Easter.

The phenomenon, understood as a whole in terms of the end-point, is interpreted and unrolled back to the beginning; the life of Jesus, understood in retrospect, is inevitably coloured over by the radiance of Easter; his claim becomes articulate as the intelligible language of God – as *theology*. And all this is perfectly legitimate, however human and time-conditioned the instruments used.

The more profoundly we reflect on the point of departure – God's corroborating the mighty claim of Jesus by his own word in raising him from the dead – the more the very origin of this claim of Jesus merges into the pre-time and supra-time of God. If his claim was valid, he must always have been (but in an incomprehensible way) what he was finally confirmed as being.

But doesn't this unique constellation – claim, cross, resurrection – break like a rogue meteorite into the horizontal course of world history? What has it to do with us? In what way has it altered the human situation? We can find a positive answer only if we first look at the Christ-event in its biblical context. If we try to bypass Paul, who in moving out to the Gentiles took with him the decisive categories of total biblical thought, we no longer understand the event.

It is a simple fact that the theology contained in the claim made by Jesus was formulated almost entirely in the language and alphabet, in the images and hieroglyphs, and in the titles and sacred nomenclature, of the Old Testament.

The shock of the fact of Easter released the locked-up treasures of the Old Testament. All the unfulfilled and arrested images and titles – Messiah, mediator, the sin-bearing servant of God, the prophet, the priest and all his sacrificial victims, the Son of Man coming on the clouds of heaven, the justice, the wisdom, and the glory of God dwelling upon earth, the Word of God, and so on – all of these at last converge by moving in upon the transcending subject who is the risen Jesus. Not until they come to rest in that which supersedes them all do they find true meaning.

b. *The second circle: the biblical event.* The Christ-event is understood as the fulfilment of all the promises of God (II Cor. 1, 19; Heb. 1, 1–2). This realization is actual, because all promises and faith in them, from the very beginning, had been aimed at resurrection from the dead.

Abraham was the first to believe the promise. He believed in a God "who brings the dead back to life and calls into being what does not exist" (Rom. 4, 17). By so doing he formulated a pattern of behaviour, and triggered off a dynamic process that was to go far beyond the symbolic confirmation of his act of faith : he received the son of promise although "his body was past fatherhood – he was about a hundred years old – and Sarah too old to become a mother" (Rom. 4, 19).

This faith in a God who can raise the dead resounds like a bass beneath all the promises to Israel. Hence the oldest Christian credal statement : "Christ died for our sins, in accordance with the Scriptures; . . . he was buried;

and . . . was raised to life on the third day, in accordance with the Scriptures" (I Cor. 15, 3 f). The whole faith of Israel is a single assault upon the frontier of death, with a dynamic that, in contrast to all other peoples, approached death not as an immovable power to be placated by some religious device or another, but as a power to be broken under all circumstances – despite the apparent resignation occasionally suggested by the Old Testament.

Proof of this may be found in present-day Jewish thought, which shows us how real this mediating second circle – the transcendence-dynamic of the Old and New covenant – is for world-history as a whole. The presupposition is the mysterious association of the two entities "law" and "death" (cf. Rom. 7). Both barriers fall together or relativize one another.

Paul puts Abraham's faith before the law that "came after", and was thus able to attribute to him a longing for a goal that lay on the other side of the law and of death. But even this faith had to supersede and depose itself, for its object is boundless, as the Letter to the Hebrews expounds, using the analogy of the superiority of Melchizedek, the immortal "king of peace" who is "like the Son of God" (Heb. 7, 3).

Israel will constantly find itself refusing to pay tithes to this mysterious king. It will try to follow three roads of escape from the dreaded gates of death and of the underworld.

1. The Platonic road leading straight up out of the

sphere of law and death into the spiritual sphere, whether in its contemplative or ethical form. This was the road followed by Josephus and Philo of Alexandria, as it is followed by idealist-liberal Jews today (Cohen and Brunschweig). But this represents a digression into the general, as we find, say, in Hegel. Death is regarded as a necessary moment in the dialectic of becoming; and it is folly for the finite individual to rush towards it. The other two schemes are to be taken more seriously.

2. Israel owed its origin to the "mighty acts of God", in which, however, it was an active and fighting participant. The prophets set the imagery of the origin (Exodus) materially in the future, making the people feel urgently their co-responsibility for the advent of the eschatological kingdom – lying temporally in the future.

The apocalyptic writers see God (in the form of his Messiahs and angel hosts) fighting with Israel in their triumphant battle against the nations. The plan of battle, which redeems Israel from all sickness, subservience, and loss of identity, is set out in the Qumran writings as "the battle of the sons of light against the sons of darkness".

Modern Marxism lives by the prophetic-apocalyptic pathos of this redemption from slavery into freedom. (The end of this development can be no other than Nikolai Federov's "philosophy of common work" [1906]: the resurrection of all past generations by means of all the elemental and technical forces of the world, so that they can share in the condition of the redeemed world.) This is linked with the zealot and Zionist inauguration of the kingdom, which for Israel, however, is to come about through Israel itself.

3. Perhaps it is unnecessary for material imagery, which in the end must always be finite and legalistic, to be projected into the future by the dynamism of prophetic, hopeful faith. Perhaps all imagery, like the law, is something that has "come after" : a transient projection of the *empty formal* drive forwards, itself creating the framework which it can then discard, and thus proving itself stronger.

It occurs (a) in the "life philosophy" (*Lebensphilosophie*) developed by the early Bergson and in detail by Simmel; (b) in the libido philosophy of Freud and his successors down to Marcuse, in open contradiction of Paul's correlation of *epithymia* (libido) with *sin* and *death*, constantly aggravated and found guilty by the *law*; (c) in Ernst Bloch's philosophy of hope, a philosophy in which the absolute drive forwards rejects the principle of legal rule from above (God).

This last idea is rooted in Job's rejection of the injustice of a God who lays upon life more of a burden of suffering than it deserves, and who appeals from this God to a transdivine court. Kafka's impeachment of the law bears an affinity to this, as does the destruction of all that has been and is, in favour of a reality that is yet to be inaugurated. (G. Landauer: "There is nothing at all; we still have to make everything.") This is perennial apocalyptic.

The presence and actuality of this unique, irrepressible

drive onwards, which stems from the Bible and rejects any assuagement from the Christ-event, becomes a lasting proof of the actuality of Jesus' claim to be the rational climax of this dynamic.

It is thus logical, and forms part of the proof of the validity of this claim, that Christians who contest the eschatological aspect of Jesus' claim, become caught up in this dynamic. For them, Jesus becomes a political theologian who at least tolerates zealots among his disciples, and by his sympathy with the people is forced to throw all human potentialities into the attempt to fulfil his mission – the coming of the kingdom of God upon earth.

In reality, however, to be the rational climax of this dynamic and to know himself as such implies that in moving towards his death (which is also the end of the world) Jesus experienced an absolute passion. His petition to God: "Thy kingdom come" contained the ultimate self-sacrifice.

It was to come through his whole life and being, through his being utterly consumed to the last drop of sweat and blood. And if it is true that the kingdom has fundamentally been reached and has come through Jesus' victory over death and his resurrection, then it has not by any means come by Jesus' sheer waiting patiently for some act to be accomplished by God alone, but by an equally impatient pressing forward towards a total effort, which then coincides with being totally used and consumed.

"I have come to bring fire upon earth. . . . There is a baptism I must still receive, and how great is my distress till it is over!" (Lk. 12, 49 f). "Learn that today and tomorrow I cast out devils and on the third day attain my end. But for today and tomorrow and the next day I must go on . . .' (Lk. 13, 32 f).

If the resurrection is not the act of the one who died (for it is the living God who raises him), then his most spiritual act and self-sacrifice enter into the resurrection as the substance which alone gives value to being raised to share the eternal life of God. "He has entered the sanctuary once and for all, taking with him . . . his own blood . . ." (Heb. 9, 12).

The difficulty of being a Christian, both in the sense of believing in Jesus and in following him is this: the passion of the Jewish before-and-after has to be taken over by the Christian, and then fulfilled as Christ fulfilled it.

The whole utopian urge towards the advent of the kingdom of God – "on earth as it is in heaven" – must, therefore, be incorporated until it includes the sacrifice of life (for if man does not offer up his life he has not given himself wholly); but sacrificing one's life to be taken over by God constitutes the ultimate renunciation of self-determination in favour of disposal by God; and such sacrifice raises the fulfilment of the claim to a dimension that lies beyond life and death.

Does this mean that all that is visible eludes the Christian, and that all his creative endeavour to mould the future of this world is always in vain? To purely im-

D

manent thinking it appears so, for then Christianity would not be the rational climax, but the abrupt cessation of movement, a betrayal of the earth.

But Jewish prophetic and apocalyptic thought goes far beyond mere immanence; it is essentially utopian. As a material projection and as formal dynamism this utopia runs into the void. It is the revelation of the goal attained : the resurrection of Jesus provides advance hope with a *real* basis. It is a *pledge* or *first instalment*, as Paul puts it. Christianity is no less utopian than Judaism, but it is *factually* utopian.

If in Jesus the fulfilment of his mission causes personal death to coincide with the accomplishment of the end of the world, that means that he must have lived through destruction and death with all men who had lived and who would live – to their final redemption.

The Old Testament category of the *"pro nobis"* (Is. 53) comes immediately to mind as a pre-Pauline interpretation of the event upon the cross. But only reflection upon the Christ-event brings to light who he must have been who could effect this *"pro nobis"*, and how he was constituted. In the claim that isolates his "I" from all other "Is" lies the power of his supreme capacity to bear so much. This is what illumines the uniqueness of his abandonment by God.

It is not just the sum, but the surpassing, of all abandonment that men could suffer. For only the I that was so close to the divine *I* – "the Word was with God . . . the Father loves the Son and shows him all that he does

. . . my food is to do the will of him who sent me" – only this "I" can know what it really means to be abandoned by God. What in the Old Testament goes by the name of "the grave", "the shades", "Sheol", stands for the enduring of utter abandonment, and corresponds to the "hell" of the New Testament, into which Jesus descended *"pro nobis"*.

c. *The third circle: the humanity-event.* On the Biblical stage, the world-historical battle about the meaning of life and of history is fought to the right and the left of the cross. The object of strife has become everything – corresponding to Jesus' original claim to be the way, the truth, and the life.

Israel remains caught in the paradox of being but one nation that was supposed, in its election, to have received an eschatological redemptive significance for all nations. This paradox – irresolvable by proselytism – is at times endured by transferring its apocalyptic restlessness to the world.

The Gospel, on the other hand, in accordance with its essence, from the very start overstepped the Biblical sphere and entered the pagan *oekumene* – the inhabited world. The claim implicit in the Gospel, that it had received and was able to proclaim all truth, was soon organically transformed into the proofs of the apologists, just as the scattered *samen-logoi* of religions and philosophies had largely to be assimilated to the eschatological synthesis of Christ.

The final task, therefore, is to prove how the claim made by Christ is a challenge to every philosophy of life – religious or secular – to measure itself against this claim, and to determine which criteria are valid in assessing the demands which Christ's claim and the philosophies make of each other.

This theme, carefully handled, would require a whole book. Only a few pointers can be given here. *Man*, as an individual and as a social animal, is seized at the core of his being by the resurrection of Christ from the dead. It is an event which completely re-values the whole of individual human life, as it does the whole of human history, since history has reached its end in the death of Jesus.

This takes place, however, only because in the Christ-event God, as Father, appears in his Son and in the communication of the Holy Spirit, so that an equally fresh concept of *God* emerges, a concept which we must take as a new starting-point if the concept of man that it determines is to achieve its full weight.

The Christian concept of God is determined by the final statements of Paul and John. These writers interpret the Christ-event theologically, and refer back to the great Old Testament election texts (e.g. Hos. 11, 8 ff; Jer. 31, 20 f; Dt. 6–7): "God loved the world so much . . . God is love." In view of the state of this world no religion other than Christianity could accept responsibility for such statements. At best God could be the peace that lies beyond mortal discord, the nothingness beyond our intolerable, meaningless existence, the world of archetypes above the reified copies. At best he could be expected to incline with compassion and grace towards suffering creatures.

But how could he ever, as Creator, accept responsibility for all the world's agony? Two things are insufficient: first, instruction, even if it did bring with it the power of overcoming suffering for oneself; for there are still the majority of those who cannot find, or are not able to walk along, these secret paths. Second, there is the thought of the power of God, to which is imputed the possibility of preserving, by a surplus of grace, the creature whom he has liberated, from apostasy from God, from guilt and its consequent disaster.

Such a God of power – even if his power were that of grace – would never have dared, or been able, seriously to give the gift of freedom to his creature. The father, whose younger son asked him for his birthright in advance so that he could go to a foreign land, did not withhold anything that was asked. Is it possible for God to lose the game of creation in the self-losing of his liberated creature? This is a profoundly mysterious possibility, for which we can find a certain human analogy, but which in the end must be consigned with relief to the realm of faith.

God goes silently along the way into complete abandonment – suffering with us, truly representing all of us. In the parable of the Prodigal Son one figure is absent: the narrator himself – Jesus. The father not only waits for the spontaneous or constrained return of the Prodigal, but (in the form of his son) sends out his love into his desolation. He allows his son to identify himself with his lost brother. And by this very power of identifying himself – without keeping a respectable distance – with his complete opposite, God the Father recognizes the *consubstantiality*, the divinity of the one he has sent as his redeeming word into the world.

He recognizes that this word, become man, has been able to do what the Father intended when he generated and uttered this word : to make himself audible and intelligible to anyone who does not want to hear any more about God. In other words : that Jesus could become the brother of the very least and of the lost; that he could reveal, more by deed than by word; that God, as all-powerful, is love, and, as love, is all-powerful; that he is this intrinsically, in the mystery of his Trinity, which can be explained only by the total opposition – between being with God and being abandoned by God – within God himself.

This mystery can reveal itself in its full reality as accompanying the sinner only *sub contrario*, in secret, because otherwise it would not have revealed itself as reality. But because in this God (and God is God only as eternal and living) reveals himself as love, he cannot have become love merely by virtue of the emancipation of the creature; he has no need of the world and its ways in order to become himself; but manifests himself, precisely in the cross of Christ, in his abandonment by God and descent into hell, as the one he always was: everlasting love.

As the three in one, God is so intensely everlasting love, that within his life temporal death and the hellish desolation of the creature, accepted out of love, can become transmuted into an expression of love. (The necessary concealment of a vicarious accompanying into abandonment also results in a certain concealment of the resurrection in the eyes of the world: an event which can be accepted only by an act of receptive faith could not become a neutral datum of world-historical publicity.)

The eschatological aspect of the Christian idea of God is that God is not immanent in all world history in a general philosophical sense, merely *because* he transcends the world and is incommensurable with it – the one with no opposite (non-aligned), the wholly other compared with all other beings who all have their opposites – but because he realizes this relationship in a way that the world cannot discover, cannot guess at, a manner that is completely free; and this manifests him as the God who in himself is absolute love (and hence a Trinity). This love cannot be elicited in restrospect by any kind of *gnosis*: everything that we can "understand" about it places us ever again before "the love of Christ, which is beyond all knowledge" (Eph. 3, 19).

Therefore the Christian concept of man is determined. Man has been endowed by God with genuine freedom and self-determination, for a work that is both himself and the world that is to be made fit for men to live in, and that is both his own human work and creative co-operation in the work of God the Creator.

Man is taken out of his depth by a naturalistically conceived immanent, or even transcendent, providence, which would relate his actions and decisions away beyond him to a goal unknown to him. Here we find limits set to all optimism concerning a court of appeal that encroaches either evolutionally or dialectically upon human freedoms.

There may be laws of the species which permit certain harmful tendencies to swing back and forth, yet which create more or less beneficial preconditions, although never determining an ultimate personal decision. We cannot rely on technical progress, for the increased power this puts in men's hands can be used both for good and for ill. Concentrations of power, moreover, offer demonic temptations to misuse them.

Neither can the dialogical principle and the communication between personal freedoms one hopes to gain from it be an escape from the loneliness of personal decision. Dialogue between individuals always has to be taken up from the beginning again, going back to the same basic questions and fundamental options. Freedom as such is not perfectible.

All the educational aids to right choice may indeed be useful, but they cannot compel; all sociological structures remain ambivalent: the proved injustice of one is no proof that another, which might redress this specific justice, will not bring with it new and perhaps greater injustices. If a State needs several hundred prisons with millions of inmates, it will hardly commend itself as a road to freedom.

Nothing can be relied upon except man himself and his freedom. But with this he would be well and truly lost if it were that solitary absolute by which he might make his way from his own nothingness either to "God" or to "the devil". Even this concept of freedom is a sign of abandonment and disorientation.

Human freedom finds a location in terms of God's freedom in Jesus Christ to accompany man vicariously into all the consequences of his abandonment. Externally this looks like mere "sharing our common humanity" – and it is that too – but it is essentially more, because this sharing our common humanity proves itself to be effective in the end in virtue of its being God-with-us. It assists us precisely at that point where mere sharing our common humanity no longer helps: in the loneliness of death, of abandonment by God, of the descent into ultimate desolation.

Jesus' companionship is not primarily earthly and humanity-sharing, in order to become eucharistic in its final phase, but is eucharistic from the very start: abandoned by God on the cross, in his broken body and shed blood, he puts himself at the disposal of his fellow men.

As fellow Christians we have carefully to assess every provisional and earthly social configuration by the principles of social justice (explicitly adopting the ethical demands of the Old Testament), yet we are always inclined to go beyond the criteria of utility and success, and to take our companionship into the darkness where earthly meaninglessness reigns.

Genuine Christian charity prefers to tend the dying, the helpless, the lepers, the mentally defective. Again: Christian compassion for men does not wish to begin, nor ought it to begin, there – thus allowing itself to be more and more ousted by increasing non-Christian welfare institutions. It begins, rather, at the heart of common, human social-welfare work, but must distinguish itself – because it knows about God's ultimate way with men – by always proceeding in tranquillity and by going on when others give up.

The impulse for the Christian to go on further is his knowledge that what is meaningless and utterly negative to the eye of man has acquired meaning through God's accompanying man in Christ. For, in Christ, the love of God has succeeded in transforming the loneliness of death and of the interrupted conversation between God and man into a situation of companionship in suffering, and of turning merely passive resignation into an expression of the most active abandonment of the self to God.

This is something unique in the whole of human thought and behaviour, for it presupposes precisely faith in the action of the triune God in the cross and resurrection of Christ. The perfect expansion of the concept of man in Christianity is correlative with the expansion of the concept of God in the Trinity and in christology.

At this point we must be prepared to face Nietzsche's reproach seriously. He said that Christianity is a religion of the weak who turn negative into positive values. It is much more the religion of those who know how to understand positively even those things which all others see as negative.

Nor must we give too much weight to Bonhoeffer's idea that Christianity ought not to address man principally in terms of his weak marginal situations, but in the concentrated strength of his existence. For it will reach the heart of the strong man only if simultaneously it permits him a glance at the periphery of existence, so that freely and positively he is able to face up to every situation – terror, sickness, weakness, loneliness, and spiritual darkness.

Today these marginal situations come into collective consciousness, hence the panic flight into anarchy and the fantasy of drugs, into artificial spirituality with its compulsive devaluation of personal freedom, its shutting its eyes to the reality of death, its destruction of childhood where the "non-adult" person can no longer rely upon loving friendship.

Teilhard de Chardin is right in asserting that Christianity alone can supply a world that doubts its capability of building up peace and contentment from its own resources, and is on the brink of giving up all hope – hence all the hysterical talk about hope – with a motive for carrying on.

7. Destruction of the Eschatological Moment

Being a Christian only makes sense if the eschatological moment of God's action in Jesus Christ is maintained. It would be meaningless if this moment were relativized and watered down so that some other factor assumed equal or greater weight.

Many people today do not realize this. Under propaganda, in face of the modern world, they concede a certain easing of burdens, and although this attitude seems tolerable it does abrogate the indivisible claim made by the Christ-event. When dealing with the primary phenomenon – the unity of Christ's claim, abandonment on the cross, and then the resurrection – the line between vitalizing re-formulation and falsification of emphasis is very hard to draw.

A decision about what is happening must be made in the clear knowledge of the absolute moment. That cannot be ascertained by any scientific measure, but must be arrived at existentially by uniting a number of considerations, and finally – if it is to be applicable – through the illumination of faith.

Who, then, is the true believer? There are many unintentional falsifiers of emphasis who in good conscience still regard themselves as believers; others, who deliberately falsify, lay great store on being thought of as believers, despite their own strong convictions. Their object very often is to deprive true believers of the eschatological basis of their faith, and to lead them into that uncertain twilight between belief and unbelief, in which they themselves dwell.

In order to "split the atom" of the complex: claim – cross – resurrection, they proceed from the weakest link in the chain, from the Easter experience of the disciples. This rests, they would argue, upon the testimony of a few people, is not verifiable, and has retrospectively affected the interpretation of the meaning of the cross and life of Jesus.

The *"pro nobis"* of the cross, its redemptive significance for mankind, is equally unverifiable; and the claim made by Jesus – supposing that the other data fall out, while the claim retains credibility – must have received considerable retrospective reinforcement. His sayings and acts have to be toned down; the miracles can easily be explained away; the imminent expectation of the kingdom can be explained in terms of contemporary atmosphere; an intensified prophetic or even Messianic mentality may have been present. The successive editing of the texts also reveals certain tendencies towards exaggeration.

Most, if not all, of the Old Testament titles were applied to Jesus only after Easter; many combinations of these titles may be found or may be taken as having been current in Jewish literature of the times. All in all, the fundamental thesis: "Jesus (the man from Nazareth) is Christ (the anointed of God and hence the fulfilment of the Old Testament eschatological promises of God to Israel and to mankind)" is an *a posteriori* synthetic proposition (Bultmann).

Despite all these arguments one must affirm that they contradict the central faith of the primitive Church, the many theological theories about which converge on the proposition "Jesus is Christ", all depend on its strength, and are inseparable from it.

They also contradict the whole Gospel of Paul, which on the one hand rests upon and is linked to the Gospel already being preached, and on the other is newly founded upon his own experience of the risen Christ, again supported upon the twin pillars of cross and resurrection, whereas for him the claim of the historical Jesus remains in the background as the presupposition that is taken for granted but not explicitly preached.

From this it becomes clear that whoever bypasses this normative phase in Christian faith by deliberately making it relative must logically renounce the term "Christ", a term which was put into the mouths of the disciples, precisely because of their common faith that Jesus was the Christ. Such a person, constructing a hypothetical Jesus of Nazareth, whose nature and doctrine remained totally obscure, might indeed call himself a "Jesusite", but he could scarcely maintain that this shadowy person and his doctrine can be a world-moving force today, certainly not a force distinguished by its eschatological moment: "*Aut Christus aut nihil.*"

A second and totally different mode of doubt is one concerned with the historical forms and effects of Christianity. This is more effective than the other, because it isolates the problem of how the incomparable One (who is also the Last), imitated by however many, can be made present down the ages.

Of necessity this has to be called in question, both in its supra-individual (institutional) aspect and in its individual (charismatic) aspect, so that the origin itself appears in a distorted light. Christians ought to look like the redeemed; the Church ought to be an image of Christ. With malicious relish we can say at once: no matter how the Church behaves it will never be able to provide a fully credible reflection of its origin in all its eschatological weight.

The answer to this is: it may never try to overlay the reality that is Christ with its own reality. With all the energy it expends in imitating and making him present it can never want to be more than a pointer towards him. And it must do this in the multiplicity of its mutually irreconcilable charisms: some turned towards the contemporary world, working in it and for it, others forward-looking and eschatological, proclaiming the coming, secretly present kingdom of God.

Without the latter, the former would run the risk of remaining stuck within the mundane sphere; without the former the latter would be tempted to flee from the demands of this present world. Christ can transmit the light of the origin only through the prism of an ecclesial togetherness; but in the prism each colour must blend with every other one.

The essence of the Church is the material love of Christians of the most diverse vocations: this loving interconnection, this transcendence of itself by each charism in allowing all the others to want, this rising of the charismatic (I Cor. 12) to a more excellent love as his foundation and goal (I Cor. 13) is the authentication of the Church's pointing to her ever-elusive origin.

There will always be people whose whole life is a convincing pointer to many others. These are "saints" in the restricted sense of the word. But these individuals are quick to declare that they could never give their testimony apart from the testimony of the Church which hands on the word and sacraments of Jesus. And if there are any who complain that the Church does not live out credibly enough that which is testified and presented in word and sacrament, they cannot wrench away from the Church that which has been entrusted to her, in order to claim it as their own monopoly.

All of this requires an exposition that would be out of place here. Let us stick to the theme of the absolute moment and end with it. The weakness of our age is that it has lost all feeling for this moment and is in danger of losing all interest in it, preferring to become wholly engrossed in the present tangible world.

One of the symptoms of this weakness is the inability of Christians to judge how much they stand to lose through the allegedly critical "reduction" of the Christian phenomenon. They no longer have eyes to see the absolute uniqueness of the claim "Jesus is Christ", and all that it implies.

They bow their necks to the yoke of a worldly reasoning that claims to grasp this unique thing, a reasoning that categorizes what is left of the mystery of Christ, thus subjecting it to a law that is no longer that of the utterly free, utterly self-abasing love of God, accompanying man in his desolation. In a frantic attempt to attract buyers, they are offering Christianity at cut prices, not realizing that by so doing they are making Christianity not of less value, but of no value at all.

Without noticing they are going the way of the Grand Inquisitor, who diffused Christianity for the masses, who must be given bread and robbed of their freedom before they are prepared to accept a faith – and what sort of faith? The Grand Inquisitor was a deliberate faker of weights; many of his imitators do not even know that they are falsifiers. They will not be taught by the Gospel, which demands of disciples not some things, but everything.

Anyone who asks so much – that a disciple give up everything to become a fisher of men – remains a sociological fool for all time. But he cannot ask less, and cannot absolve from the utmost effort, without denying that he "is it" : the way, the truth, and the life.

E

That which demands most is also the most beautiful. Because it is love, the hardest proves to be a "light burden, an easy yoke"; it is what, despite much resistance, in the end a man does most willingly.

On the human level, love is just one of the possibilities arising from freedom. On the divine level, love becomes *the* manifestation of divine freedom, proven in the claim, cross and resurrection of Christ, where alone being can itself be loved as love. As love, it embraces and supports man's becoming and dissolution, so that his strength and helplessness alike become meaningful and lovable.

The point from which all this light shines out is the intersection between God and the world: a point called Jesus Christ. He is not only a more or less accidental occasion for a universal doctrine and system of truth but the lasting manifestation of divine and human love together – its actuality and focus in the deepest sense.

The Holy Spirit of God is able to take our lives to that point, but we never become identified with him so that he ceases to be the highest object of our love – a "thou" who shines forth meaningfully and clearly to us, as the inscrutable "thou" of the threefold God of Love, and as the constantly reappearing "thou" of the "least of these my brothers".

Today there are many and contradictory reasons for no longer remaining in the Church. To turn one's back on the Church is an urge felt not only by those alienated from the faith of the Church, by men to whom the Church appears out-of-date, medieval, too much at enmity with life and the world, but also by those who loved the historical form of the Church, its worship, agelessness and the reflection in it of the eternal.

To them it seems as though the Church is betraying its essential nature, selling out to the way of the world and losing its soul. They are disillusioned, like any lover whose great love has been betrayed; in all seriousness they dare to turn their backs on the Church.

On the other hand, there are quite contradictory reasons for staying in the Church. Not only those stay who are immovable in their faith in the Church's mission, or who do not want to break with an old beloved habit – even if they make little use of it – but those who disavow the Church's whole historical manifestion, and vehemently attack the substance which church officials try to keep in or infuse into it.

The second group are often the more zealous; although they want to discard what the Church was and is, they are determined not to be expelled from it, so that they can make of it what they think it is intended to become.

1. Introductory Thoughts on the State of the Church

The Church now finds itself in a situation of Babylonian captivity, in which the "for" and "against" attitudes are not only tangled up in the oddest ways, but seem to allow scarcely any reconciliation. Mistrust has emerged, because being in the Church has lost straightforwardness and no one any longer risks attributing honesty to another.

Romano Guardini's hopeful observance of 1921 (A process of great moment has begun, the Church is coming to life in the souls of men) seems to have turned into its opposite. Today the saying would seem to run thus: Indeed, momentous things are in progress, the Church is becoming extinguished in men's souls, and Christian communities are crumbling. In the midst of a world striving for unity the Church is falling apart in nationalistic partisanship, in calumniation of the alien and glorification of self.

There seems to be no middle way between the iconoclasts and a reaction that clings too much to externals and what always has been, between contempt of tradition and a mechanical dependence on the letter. Public opinion places everyone inexorably in his precise category, for it needs to have clear-cut rules, and admits of no nuances : a person has to be either a progressive or a conservative. But reality, however, is different.

Silently, with no voice to speak for them, even at this time of confusion, the simple faithful carry on fulfilling the Church's true mission : prayer, bearing daily life with patience, always listening to the word of God. But they do not fit into the picture that people want to see; and so, for the most part, they remain silent, although this Church is by no means invisible, though hidden deep beneath the powers of this world.

So far we have discovered our first clue about the background against which we must ask : Why am I still in the Church ? In order to find a meaningful answer we have first of all to scrutinize this background. which is linked directly to our topic by the little word "today", and, having described the situation, go on further to seek for its causes.

How was it possible for this Babylonian captivity to arise at a moment when we had been hoping for a new Pentecost ? How was it possible that just when the Council seemed to have reaped the ripe harvest of the last decades, instead of enjoying the riches of fulfilment we found only emptiness ? How could disintegration emerge from a great surge towards unity ?

For a start, I shall try to reply with a metaphor designed both to clarify the task before us and to begin to reveal how it is possible for every No to contain a Yes.

It would seem that in our efforts to understand the Church, efforts which at the Council finally developed into an active struggle for the Church, and into concrete work upon the Church, we have come so close to the Church that we can no longer see it as a whole : we cannot see the city for the houses, or the wood for the trees.

The situation into which science has so often led us in respect of reality seems now to have arisen in respect of the Church. We can see the detail with such precision that we cannot see the whole thing. As in scientific study, so here, an increment in exactitude represents loss in truth. Indisputably precise as is all that the microscope shows when we look through it at a section from a tree, it may obscure truth if it makes us forget that the individual is not just an individual, but has life within the whole, which is not visible under the microscope and yet is true – truer, indeed, than the isolation of the individual.

The perspective of the present day has distorted our view of the Church, so that in practice we see the Church only under the aspect of adaptability, in terms of what can be made of it. Intensive efforts to reform the Church have caused everything else to be forgotten.

For us today the Church is only a structure that can be changed, and which constantly causes us to ask what can be altered, in order to make the Church more efficient for the functions that someone or other thinks appropriate. In all this questioning the concept of reform as it occurs in the popular mind has largely degenerated and lost its essence.

Reform originally meant a spiritual process, very much akin to repentance. A man becomes a Christian only by repenting; and that applies throughout his life; it applies to the Church throughout its history. The Church, too, keeps alive as the Church by turning again and again to its Lord, by fighting ossification and comfortable habits which so easily fall into antagonism to the truth.

When reform is dissociated from the hard work of repentance, and seeks salvation merely by changing others, by creating ever fresh forms, and by accommodation to the times, then despite many useful innovations it will be a caricature of itself. Such reform can touch only things of secondary importance in the Church.

No wonder, then, that in the end it sees the Church itself as of secondary importance. If we become aware of this, the paradox that has emerged apparently with the present efforts at reform becomes intelligible : the attempt to loosen up rigid structures, to correct forms of Church government and ministry, which derive from the Middle Ages, or, rather, the age of absolutism, and to liberate the Church from such encrustations and inaugurate a simpler ministry in the spirit of the Gospel – all these efforts have led to an almost unparalleled over-emphasis on the official elements in the Church.

It is true that today the institutions and ministries in the Church are being criticized more radically than ever before, but in the process they attract more exclusive attention than ever before.

For not a few people the Church today seems to consist of nothing but these. And so, questions about the Church exhaust themselves in a battle about machinery; one does not want to leave such an elaborate piece of mechanism lying about idle, yet finds it wholly unsuited to the new functions it is expected to fulfil.

Behind this the real problem appears: the crisis of faith which is the true heart of the process. The sociological radius of the Church still extends far beyond the circle of the genuine faithful.

The publicity effect of the Council and the apparent possibility of *rapprochement* between belief and unbelief – an illusion fostered almost inevitably by the popular new coverage given to the Council – pushed this alienation to the limit.

Applause for the Council came in part from those who had no intention of becoming believers, in the traditional Christian sense, but who hailed the "progress" of the Church in the direction of their own views, taking this as a corroboration of their way of life. It is true that at the same time in the Church itself faith is in a state of ferment.

The problem of historical transmission sets the ancient creed in a doubtful twilight in which outlines become blurred; the objections of science or, rather, of what people think is the modern view of the world, play a part in making the process worse.

The boundary-line between interpretation and falsification, even at the very heart of things, becomes more and more confused. What do we really mean by "resurrection from the dead"? Who is believing, who is interpreting, who is falsifying? The countenance of God rapidly disappears behind this argument about the limits of interpretation. The "death of God" is a very real process, and today reaches right into the heart of the Church. It looks as if God were dying within Christianity. For where the resurrection becomes the experience of a message that is felt to be cast in out-of-date imagery, God ceases to be at work.

Does he work at all? This is the question that follows immediately. But who is so reactionary as to insist upon a realistic "He is risen"? And what one sees as progress another thinks of as unbelief, and what was for aeons inconceivable is now usual: men who have long since given up the Church's creed, in good conscience regard themselves as genuine progressive Christians.

For them the one standard by which to judge the Church is the efficiency with which it operates. Obviously we have to ask what efficiency is, and what the end is which it subserves. Is it supposed to provide a critique of society, to assist evolution, or to inaugurate revolution, Or is it there to promote community celebrations? At all events we have to start again from the ground floor, for the Church was originally designed for none of these things, and in its present form really is not adapted to these functions at all.

Discontent grows among believers and unbelievers alike. The foothold gained by unbelief within the Church makes the situation seem intolerable to both parties; most of all, these circumstances have given the reform programme a certain notable ambiguity, which to many seems almost irremovable – at least for the time being.

Quite obviously this is not the whole story. In recent years many positive things have happened, about which we must not keep silent: the new accessibility of the liturgy, an awareness of social problems, a better understanding between separated Christians, the removal of much anguish that had arisen from a false and liberalistic faith, and many other things.

All this is true and not to be minimized. But these things are not the distinguishing features of the general climate in the Church. On the contrary, all of this has in the meantime passed into the twilight created by the blurring of the lines of demarcation between faith and unbelief. Only at the beginning did this blurring look like a liberation. Today it is clear that, in spite of all signs of hope, the Church that has emerged from this process is not a modern but a thoroughly shaky and deeply divided Church.

Let us put it very crudely: the first Vatican Council described the Church as a *"signum levatum in nationes"*, as the great eschatological banner that was visible from afar and called and united men. It was (so said the Council of 1870) that for which Isaiah had hoped (Is. 11, 12): the universally visible sign that every man could recognize and that pointed the way unequivocally to all men. With its astounding expansion, superb holiness, fecundity in all goodness, and invincible stability, it was supposed to be the real miracle of Christianity, its permanent authentication – replacing all other signs and miracles – in the eyes of history.[2]

Today everything seems to have turned to the opposite. There is no marvellous expansion, but only a small-scale, stagnating association that cannot seriously overstep the boundaries of Europe or of the spirit of the Middle Ages; there is no superb holiness, but a collection of all human sicknesses besmirched and humiliated by a history from which no scandal is absent – the persecution of heretics and witch-hunting, persecution of the Jews and violation of conscience, self-dogmatizing and opposition to scientific evidence – so that anyone who listens to this story can only cover his head in shame; there is no stability, but only involvement in all the streams of history, in colonialism and nationalism, and the beginnings of adaptation to, and even identification with, Marxism. These are not signs that evoke faith, but seem to constitute a supreme obstacle to it.

A true theology of the Church would seem to consist in denuding the Church of all theological attributes and looking on it as a wholly political entity. Then it is no longer seen as a reality of faith, but as a purely accidental – even if indispensable – organization of the faithful, which ought as quickly as possible to be remodelled according to the most recent sociological theory. Trust is good, but control is better – after all our disillusionment with the official Church; this is now our slogan. The sacramental principle is no longer self-evident; the only reliable thing is democratic control.[3]

Ultimately we come to the point where the Holy Spirit himself is also incomprehensible. Anyone who is unafraid to look back into the past is aware, of course, that the scandals of history arose from the conviction that man must always seize power, that only the achievements of power are real.

2. An Image of the Essence of the Church

A Church seen against the background of its whole history and its very essence as purely political makes no sense. To give a wholly political reason for staying in the Church is dishonest, even if it seems quite sincere. How then, in view of the contemporary situation, can remaining in the Church be justified? The decision for the Church must be a spiritual decision if it is to make sense; but how can such a spiritual decision be substantiated?

I would like to give an initial answer in the form of a metaphor, and refer back to what I said in describing the present situation. I said that in dealing with the Church we had come so close to it, that we could no longer see it as a whole. This statement can be expanded if we adopt an image used by the Fathers of the Church in their symbolic descriptions of the world and the Church.

In the structure of the universe, so they explain, the moon is the analogue of that which the Church is in the scheme of redemption, in the intellectual and spiritual universe. This goes back to primeval religious symbolism (the Fathers said nothing about the "theology of religions" but they made full use of it) in which the moon, symbol of fecundity as of weakness, of death and dissolution as of hope in rebirth and resurrection, became a symbol of human life – "at once pathetic and comforting".[4]

Lunar and telluric symbolism frequently intermingle. In its transitoriness as in its rebirth the moon represents the world of men, the earth, the world that is characterized by passivity and privation, receiving its fecundity from elsewhere – from the sun. Lunar symbolism becomes both a symbol for man and for humanity as represented by woman, who is passive and fruitful from the power of what she receives.

The transference of moon-symbolism to the Church was suggested to the Fathers by two things: the association of the moon with woman (mother) and the fact that the light of the moon is borrowed light, the light of Helios, without which the moon would be darkness. The moon shines, yet its light is not its own, but the light of another.[5] It is darkness and light both at once. In itself it is darkness, but it sends out light from another whose light is transmitted through it.

It is precisely in this that it represents the Church, which shines even although it is itself darkness: not with its own light is it bright, but it receives light from the true Helios who is Christ, so that although of earthly stuff itself (just as the moon is another earth) none the less in the night of our estrangement from God it can give light – "the moon speaks to us of the mystery of Christ".[6]

Symbolism must not be pressed too far. Its value consists precisely in the pictorial quality that eludes logical schematization. However, in this age of journeys to the moon, we are almost obliged to take the comparison further, and, in the antithesis between physical and symbolic thinking, to see the specific quality of our situation vis-à-vis the reality that is the Church.

The travellers to the moon explore the moon merely as rock, desert, sand, mountains, and so on, but never as light. In itself, moreover, that is all that it is: desert, sand, rock. And yet it is, not intrinsically, but from another point of view, light, and continues to be light even in this age of space-travel. It is that which it is not in itself. The other, that which is not its own, is none the less its reality – as not its own.

There is a truth of physics and there is a truth of poetry, of symbolism, and the one does not destroy the other. Now we ask: is that not a very accurate picture of the Church? If one travels around it and digs it up with the techniques of the space-traveller, one finds only deserts, sand, and rocks – the human qualities of man and his history, with its deserts, its dust, and its heights. That is proper to it. And yet that is not the most characteristic thing about it. The decisive thing is that although it is intrinsically no more than sand and stone, it is also light from the Lord, from someone other than itself.

The essence of the Church is that it counts for nothing in itself, in that the thing about it that counts is what it is not, in that it exists only to be dispossessed, in that it possesses a light that it is not and because of which alone it nonetheless is. The Church is the moon – the *mysterium lunae* – and thus exists for the faithful, for thus it is the place of an enduring spiritual decision.

Because the material touched on in this imagery seems to me decisive, I would like, before trying to translate it into factual language, to clarify it with another observation. After the liturgy had been translated into the vernacular, before the last reform, I always experienced verbal embarrassment over a particular text, which is connected with the very things we have just been discussing.

In the German version of the *Suscipiat* the Lord was asked to accept the sacrifice "as a blessing for us and all *his* holy Church". I was always on the point of saying "and all *our* holy Church".

This verbal embarrassment brings to light the whole problem. His Church has been replaced by our Church, and hence by the many Churches – for everyone has his own. The Churches have become *our* enterprises, of which we are proud or else ashamed.

Many small private properties are ranged alongside one another – nothing but *our* Churches, made by ourselves, our own work and property, and which we want to keep as they are or refashion as we think fit.

Behind *our* Church or *your* Church *his* Church has

F

3. Why I Stay in the Church

Now we have already given the main answer to the question. I am in the Church, because I believe that now as formerly, and inexorably through us, behind *our Church his Church* lives, and that I cannot remain with him except by remaining in his Church. I am in the Church because, in spite of everything, I believe that at the deepest level it is not our, but his, Church.

In concrete terms that means: it is the Church that, in spite of all the human frailty in it, gives Jesus Christ to us, and only through it are we able to receive him as a living, all-powerful reality, who challenges me and endows me here and now.

Henri de Lubac states this fact in the following way: "Don't those who accept Jesus while rejecting his Church know that in the last analysis they have the Church to thank for him? . . . For us Jesus is living. But under which sandhill would, perhaps not his name or memory, but his living influence, the effect of the Gospel and of faith in his divine person, lie buried, were it not for the continuity of his Church? 'Without the Church Christ would be bound to evaporate, crumble, become extinguished.' And what would mankind be, were Christ to have been taken from them?"

This elementary fact must stand right at the beginning. Whatever faithlessness there has been or will be in the Church, no matter how true it is that it must for ever reassess itself by the measure of Christ, there is no ultimate opposition between Christ and the Church. It is through the Church that he goes on living across the span of the centuries, that he speaks to us, that he is united to us today as Master and Lord, as our brother, making us all brothers and sisters of one another.

And because the Church alone gives Jesus Christ to us and makes him present and alive in the world, gives birth to him anew in the faith and prayer of men in all ages, it gives mankind a light, a resting-place and a measuring-rod, without which life would be unthinkable. Whoever wants Christ to be present in mankind will not find him there against the Church, but only in it.

This brings us to the next theme. I am in the Church for the same reasons that make me a Christian. A man can't believe all on his own, but only as one among fellow believers. Faith is essentially the power of union. Its archetype is the story of Pentecost : the miracle of understanding that arises between men who, by descent and history, are strangers to one another. Faith occurs in the Church or not at all.

And just as a man cannot believe all on his own, but only as one of a number of fellow believers, so he cannot believe through his own power and discovery, but only if and because the capacity for faith is given; and this is not in a man's power to give: it does not come from his own strength, but comes to meet him from outside.

A self-acquired faith is a self-contradiction; for such a faith could only guarantee and tell me what I am and know without it; it could never break through the frontiers of my own ego. A self-made Church, a community that creates itself, that exists by its own graces, is likewise a self-contradiction. If faith requires a community it must be one that possesses a power that comes to meet me, not one that is my own creation or the instrument of my own desires.

All of this can be formulated from a more historical angle. Either Jesus was more than mere man and hence possessed a power that was more than the product of a human will, and this power proceeded from him and endured right through the ages, or he left behind no such power at all.

In that case I would have to rely entirely on my own reconstruction, and he would be no more than another great religious founder, to be made present in later generations by the process of reflection. But if he is more than that he will not be dependent upon my reconstruction, and the power he left behind will be operative today also.

To recapitulate : a man can be a Christian only in the Church, not outside it. We have to ask quite soberly : What would the world be without Christ, without a

God who speaks and knows men, and whom, therefore, men can come to know?

Today we know where the attempt to run such a world is being made with such dogged tenacity. We know exactly what that means: an experiment in absurdity; an experiment with no measuring-rod. However often actual Christianity may have failed in the course of history – and it has failed lamentably, and over and over again – the standards of justice and love have come, sometimes against the will of Christians, from the Gospel it preached, and often in judgment of Christians themselves. And these standards have never failed to exercise the silent power of the one who lives behind them.

I stay in the Church because I recognize the faith that in the end we can acquire only in the Church, and not in opposition to it, as a necessity for men and for the world, for by this the world lives, even when it does not share it. For where God no longer is (and a silent God is no God at all) there no longer is the truth which leads on in front of men and the world.

But man cannot go on living in a world without truth; when man denies himself truth he ekes out an existence on the illusion that the light of truth has not yet been extinguished, just as the sun's light would last for a while after it had ended so that we would be deceived about the universal night that had come upon us.

The same thing can be formulated from yet another angle. I remain in the Church, because only the Church's faith can redeem mankind. This sounds terribly traditional, dogmatic, unreal, and yet it is said soberly, and meant to be taken realistically. In our world of stresses and frustrations there has been a resurgence, with elemental force, of the longing for redemption.

The work of Freud and C. G. Jung is only an attempt to bring redemption to the unredeemed. In their own ways and from different presuppositions, Marcuse, Adorno and Habermas carry on seeking for and proclaiming redemption. In the background stands Karl Marx, and his question, too, is about redemption. The freer, the more enlightened, the more powerful man becomes, the more he is caught up by the longing for redemption, the less free he feels himself to be.

All these efforts, from Marx to Marcuse, have been a search for redemption by striving to build a world free from pain, sickness, and sorrow. A world free from tyranny, pain, and injustice has become the great slogan of our generation. The violent explosions of youth proclaim this promise, and the angry resentment of the old is a complaint that the promise remains unfulfilled, because there still are tyranny, injustice, and pain.

To fight against pain and injustice in the world is a thoroughly Christian impulse. But to imagine that one can inaugurate a sorrow-free world through social reform and the abolition of government and the rule of law, and the demand that this be accomplished here and now, represent an erroneous doctrine, a serious error concerning the nature of man.

In this world sorrow and pain do not arise from an

inequality of possessions or power. And pain is not the only burden that man has to shake off. Whoever thinks like that must flee into the bestiality of narcotics, there well and truly to destroy himself and fall into contradiction with reality. Only in suffering himself, and in "suffering himself free" from the tyranny of egotism does man find his truth, his peace, and his happiness.

Today an illusion is dangled before us: that a man can find himself without first conquering himself, without the patience of self-denial, and the labour of self-control, that there is no need to endure the discomfort of upholding tradition, or to continue suffering the tension between the ideal and the actual in our nature.

The presentation of this illusion constitutes the real crisis of our times. A man who has been relieved of all tribulation and led off into a never-never land has lost what makes him what he is, has lost himself.

In truth man will be redeemed only through the cross, through accepting his own and the world's passion. which, in the passion of God has become the place of liberating meaning. Only thus, by this acceptance, does man become free. All cheaper offers will fail and reveal themselves as deceits.

The hope of Christianity, the opportunity of faith, in the end rests simply upon the fact that it speaks the truth. The opportunity of faith is the opportunity of truth, which can become obscured and downtrodden, but never totally destroyed.

And so we come to the final point. A man always sees

only to the extent that he loves. True, there is a clear-sightedness of denial and of hate. But these can see only what is commensurate with themselves : negativity. They are thus able to preserve love from a blindness in which it fails to see her own limitations and dangers. But they cannot be constructive.

Whoever does not commit himself at least a little to the experiment of faith, to the positive experiment of the Church, who does not risk looking about him with the eyes of love, will only distress himself. The venture of love is the precondition of faith. If a man makes this venture, he has no need to shut his eyes to the darkness in the Church. But he will discover, too, that there is more there than dark spots.

He will discover that besides the history of scandals in the Church there is a history, too, of liberating grace which throughout all the centuries has been kept fruit-fully alive in major figures like Augustine, Francis of Assisi, the Dominican Las Casas with his passionate fight for the Indios, Vincent de Paul, and John XXIII. He will find that the Church has carried down the corridors of history a lighted torch that cannot be extinguished, and that cannot be ignored.

The beauty, likewise, that has been engendered at the impulse of the Gospel, and which is manifest still today in many incomparable works of art, provides another witness to the truth. Anything that is able to express itself so, cannot be wholly dark. The beauty of the great cathedrals, the beauty of the music that has grown up around the faith, the dignity of the Church's liturgy, most of all the reality of festival – a thing that man cannot contrive for himself, but only be given[7] – the transmutation of the year into the Christian Year, in which the past and the present, time and eternity, intermingle – all of this, as I see it, is certainly no meaningless accident.

Beauty is the radiance that shines out from truth, as Aquinas once said, and, one might add, the caricature of beauty is the self-irony of lost truth. The expression which faith has been able to achieve of itself in history bears witness for it of the truth which stands behind it.

There is one further piece of evidence that I would not like to omit, even though it seems to lead well into subjectivity. Even today, if one keeps one's eyes open, one can meet men who are living witnesses to the liberating power of Christian faith. There is no shame in being a Christian in the company of these men who set before us a model of what it is to be a Christian; in their lives they make being a Christian something credible and delightful.

In the end it is sheer illusion for a man to want to turn himself into a kind of transcendental subject, in which only the absolute counts for anything. Certainly it is a duty for us to reflect upon such experiences, to test their reliability, to purify them and fulfil them anew.

But even in this necessary process of objectification surely we find a respectable demonstration of Christianity, a demonstration that it has made men human by uniting them with God. Does not something most subjective turn out to be at the same time wholly objective, and something we need feel ashamed of before no man?

One observation in conclusion. If we say, as we did, that without love a man can see nothing, that men must, therefore, love the Church if they are to recognize it, then many today will become uneasy. Is not love the antithesis of criticism? And in the end isn't it used as an excuse by the establishment to stifle criticism and maintain the *status quo*? Do we serve men by calming them down and whitewashing things as they are, or do we serve them by constantly taking up arms against entrenched injustice and against the dominant structures of society?

These are very far-reaching questions that we cannot discuss in detail here. One thing, however, ought to be clear: true love is neither static nor uncritical. If there is any chance at all of changing another man positively, then it can be done only by loving him and so helping him to change gradually from what he is into that which he is capable of becoming. And can it be otherwise with the Church? Look at very recent history: in the liturgical and theological revival of the first half of this century there was a genuine reform which achieved positive change.

This was possible because there were wide-awake men who, with the gift of discernment, loved the Church "critically", and were ready to suffer for it. If today nothing more is achieved, that may well be because we are all too set on proving our own point. To remain in a Church

Notes

1. The lecture-form of this paper and the nature of the topic set me make an exhaustive exposition of the objective reasons for being in the Church impossible. All I can do is to put together a few indications of the reasons behind what, in the end, is a very personal decision. In their own way, however, these hints and suggestions will no doubt reveal something of the objective validity of such a decision.

2. Denzinger-Schönmezer, *Enchiridion Symbolorum* (Freiburg, 1963), no. 3013 f.

3. The viewpoint that such aspirations contain legitimate elements, which over a wide area are perfectly compatible with the sacramentally determined form of church government, is expounded, with the requisite distinctions, in J. Ratzinger & H. Maier, *Demokratie in der Kirche* (Limburg, 1970).

4. Mircea Eliade, *Patterns in Comparative Religion* (London & New York, 1958), p. 184; cf. in general the whole chapter, "The Moon and its Mystique", pp. 154–87.

5. Cf. Hugo Rahner, *Greek Myths and Christian Mystery* (London, 1963), pp. 89–176, and *Symbole der Kirche* (Salzburg, 1964), pp. 89–173. It is interesting to note that in the ancient world they discussed whether the moon's light was its own or borrowed. For the most part, the Fathers opted for the second idea and made symbolic use of it in theology.

6. Ambrose, *Exameron* IV 8, 23 CSEL 32, 1 p. 137, Z 27 f; H. Rahner, *Greek Myths and Christian Mystery*, op. cit., pp. 154 ff.

7. Cf. esp. J. Pieper, *Leisure the Basis of Culture* (London, 1948).

Biographical Notes

Dr. Hans Urs von Balthasar was born in Lucerne on August 12, 1905. After studies in German language and culture, in theology and philosophy, in Vienna, Berlin, and Zürich, in 1929 he received the degree of D.Phil. For many years he has been active as an author and as director of the Johannes-Verlag in Basle. He has written many books on religion, aesthetics and literature.

Prof. Dr. Joseph Ratzinger was born in Marktl/Inn on April 16, 1927. After studies in philosophy and theology in Freising and Munich he received the degree of D.Theol. in 1953. Since his appointment in 1957 as tutor and professor he has worked in Munich, Freising, Bonn, Münster, and Tübingen. Since 1969 he has been professor of dogmatics at the university of Regensburg. He was a *peritus* at the Second Vatican Council. He is the author of numerous theological works.